TIMOTHY OF THE CAY

by
Theodore Taylor

Teacher Guide

Written by:
Anne Troy

Note
The Avon Flare paperback edition of the book was used to prepare this teacher guide. The page references may differ in the hardcover or other paperback editions.

ISBN 1-56137-742-2

To order, contact your local school
supply store, or—

Table of Contents

Skills and Strategies

Thinking
Brainstorming

Literary Elements
Dialect, colloquialism,
point of view, mood,
characterization, story
elements, conflict

Comprehension
Predicting, comparison/
contrast

Writing
Reading response log,
description, dialogue,
creative narrative

Vocabulary
Sorting, word mapping

Listening/Speaking
Dialogue, interviewing
discussion

Summary of Timothy of the Cay

In *Timothy of the Cay*, Theodore Taylor explores both the black man Timothy's life as it leads up to the torpedoing of the *Hato* in the Caribbean during WW II, and 12-year-old Phillip Enright's journey back to civilization after his rescue from the island. Alternating chapters follow Timothy from his early abandonment by his mother, through his struggles to sail the sea and his command of his own ship; and Phillip's agony as he returns to life with his parents, through an operation to regain his sight, and finally to a return with his father to Timothy's cay. Timothy's chapters sketch a world of racial prejudice. In Phillip's chapters, the reader, along with Phillip, recognizes his mother's prejudices and sees the world with new clarity in his world of blindness.

About the Author

Theodore Taylor was born June 23, 1921, in Statesville, North Carolina. He attended the U.S. Merchant Marine Academy, Kings Point, New York, and Columbia University. He also studied at the American Theatre. He has been a reporter, sportswriter, publicist, story editor, and assistant producer. He has been a full-time writer since 1961.

Taylor says of himself, "The first stories that I recall were mainly Bible stories. Action was what I liked, and I still prefer action stories, both to read and to write. I never was a very good student. When I should have been listening to the teacher, I filled sheets of paper with war scenes. It was after school that I excelled in the practice of freedom. I roamed the fields and muddy creeks and other interesting places around and about town. My mother trusted in God that I'd always be safe. I had remarkable freedom for a kid curious about most things."

Taylor began writing at the age of 13 as a cub reporter for the Portsmouth, Virginia *Evening Star*. He covered the high school sports events, and was paid 50 cents a week for his weekly sports column. This started him on a newspaper writing career. He had a stint with the Merchant Marines, and then the United States Navy. He and his family moved to California in 1955, where Taylor worked in Hollywood for the next 13 years as a publicist, story editor, associate producer and free-lance press agent. His first children's book, *People Who Make Movies*, was published in 1967.

For relaxation, Taylor enjoys walking along the beach, and traveling. He works on his various writing projects, often working on two or three novels at once, in his office every day. He works eight hours a day, seven days a week, except during football season. Then, he works five days a week.

Introductory Activities and Information

Note:
It is not intended that everything presented in this guide be done. Please be selective, and use discretion when choosing the activities you will do with the unit. The choices that are made should be appropriate for your use and your group of students. A wide range of activities has been provided so that individuals as well as groups may benefit.

Initiating Activities:
To the Teacher: Use one or more of the following prereading activities to help students draw from their background knowledge about the events and themes they will meet in *Timothy of the Cay*.

1. Predictions: Have students examine the cover illustration and title. Ask what predictions they have about the book. Some prompts include: What is a cay? *(A cay is a small, low islet composed of sand and coral.)* Does the picture on the cover give you any clues as to why this book is called *Timothy of the Cay*? Is Timothy the boy or the older man? What does the palm tree indicate? Read the back cover. How many of you have read *The Cay*? What do you think a prequel-sequel is? (See the next page of this guide.)

2. Discussion: Ask students the questions following each topic. They might work in groups to formulate answers. Alternatively, use the questions as a prereading writing assignment.

   *On Friendship: What qualities do you look for in a friend? Do friends have to be about the same age? Does a difference in race or sex make a difference in friendship? How do friends hurt one another? What do you do for a friend?

   *On World War II: What do you know about World War II? What was going on during the summer of 1942? What impact do you think the world events had on a typical 12-year-old at that time?

   *Growing Up: What does that phrase mean? Are you experiencing "growing up" right now? What's hard about it? What are some of the pluses? How do you know when you have finally "grown up"? What are some of the circumstances that force young people to grow up in a hurry? At what age do you think you will be considered grown up?

Using Predictions in the Novel Unit Approach

We all make predictions as we read—little guesses about what will happen next, how the conflict will be resolved, which details given by the author will be important to the plot, which details will help to fill in our sense of a character. Students should be encouraged to predict, to make sensible guesses. As students work on predictions, these discussion questions can be used to guide them: What are some of the ways to predict? What is the process of a sophisticated reader's thinking and predicting? What clues does an author give us to help us in making our predictions? Why are some predictions more likely than others?

A predicting chart is for students to record their predictions. As each subsequent chapter is discussed, you can review and correct previous predictions. This procedure serves to focus on predictions and to review the stories.

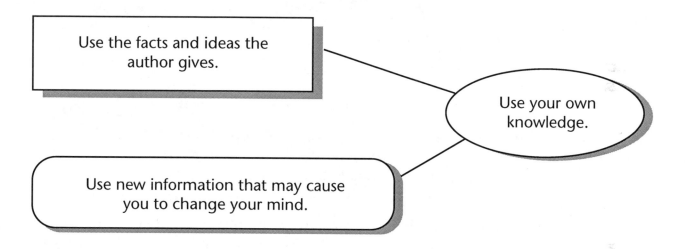

Prediction Chart

What characters have we met so far?	What is the conflict in the story?	What are your predictions?	Why did you make those predictions?

3. Brainstorming: Write the word "Blind" at the center of a large piece of butcher paper or on the board. Have students say whatever comes to mind as you jot their ideas around the word. Help students "cluster" the ideas into categories.

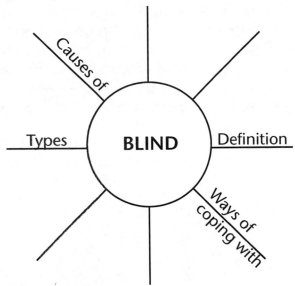

4. Log: Have students keep a response log as they read.

*In one type of log, the student assumes the persona of one of the characters. Writing on one side of each piece of paper, the student writes in the first person ("I...") about his/her reactions to what happened in the chapter. A partner (or the teacher) responds to these writings on the other side of the paper, as if talking to the character.

*In the dual entry log, students jot down brief summaries and reactions to each section of the novel they have read. (The first entry could be made based on a preview of the novel—a glance at the cover and a flip through the book.)

Pages	Summary	Reactions
		These might begin: This book is exciting because...
		This makes me think of the time...
		Phillip is selfish and self-centered but...
		I am like Phillip in some ways...

Alternatively, students might simply jot responses on "sticky notes" for reference during discussions.

5. *Timothy of the Cay* is an example of a realistic/problem novel. In realistic fiction, characters are usually creations of the writer's imagination. The setting is real—usually a time and a place in the twentieth century. Help students fill in the chart comparing and contrasting fantasy fiction with realistic fiction.

	Realistic Fiction	Fantasy Fiction
Setting:	Our world	Can almost be our world but with some unusual things
Characters:	People like us	Some characters may be like us but there are unusual characters
Action:	Could happen	Could not happen
Problem:	Could be ours	Never could be ours
Example:	*Where the Red Fern Grows*	*Wrinkle in Time*

6. Story Map: Many stories have the same parts—a setting, a problem, a goal, and a series of events that leads to an ending or conclusion. *Timothy of the Cay* is an unusual book because the various chapters have different time settings, which challenge the reader. A large sequence chart will help students, as well as the story map, to sort out the story. (See page 9 of this guide.) The story elements may be placed on the story map as the book is read. (See pages 10-11 of this guide.)

Teacher Information:
Ship Terminology:

page 6, *Knot:* One nautical mile per hour equivalent to 1.156 statute miles per hour.

page 8, *Schooner:* A fore-and-aft rigged vessel having two or more masts.
Bark: A sailing vessel with three or more masts.
Sloop: A single masted, fore-and-aft rigged sailing vessel carrying at least one jib.

page 10, *Bollard:* A vertical post, as on a wharf, for securing ropes.

page 11, *Mainmast:* A vertical spar set in a ship. Its prime use is to carry sails.
Mizzenmast: In a ship with three masts, the mast nearest the stern, from the forward end of the ship.

page 34, *Stern:* The back or rear part of a ship.

page 37,   *Ballast*: Any heavy substance, as sand, stone, etc., laid in the hold of a vessel to steady it.

page 75,   *Aftermast*: Mast toward the stern.
Jibs: A triangular sail set by sailing vessels on the stays of the foremast.

page 76,   *Forecastle*: The forward part of a merchant ship where the sailors live.
Bulkhead: An upright partition in a vessel separating compartments.
Galley: The ship's kitchen.

page 77,   *Halyard*: A rope or cable used for mooring, towing, etc.

page 78,   *Log*: A daily record of a ship's progress.
Crosstrees: Pieces of wood or metal set crosswise at the head of a mast to sustain the top or to extend the topgallant shrouds.

page 82,   *Ratline*: One of a series of rope steps up the shrouds of a mast by which men working aloft in the square-rigged ships reach the yards via the tops and crosstrees.

page 90,   *Holystone*: A flat piece of soft sandstone used to scour the wooden decks of a ship.
Shrouds: One of the ropes leading from the masthead of a ship to the side to support the mast.

page 91,   *Royal*: Sail next above the topgallant, used in a light breeze.

page 112, *Taffrail*: Rail around a vessel's stern; the upper part of a vessel's stern.

page 119, *Helm*: A lever or wheel for steering a ship; a position of control.

page 120, *Barometer*: An instrument for measuring atmospheric pressure, used in forecasting weather.

page 137, *Fantail*: The overhanging stem of some ships.
Fore: At or toward the bow of a ship.
Aft: Near the rear or stern of the ship.

Suggestion: Have students make a large ship or post a picture of a large ship on the bulletin board and mark the appropriate location for each term as it is met in the story. Students may enjoy research on sailing ships of the 19th century. See Bibliography. (page 38 of this guide)

Sequence Chart

Directions: This novel begins in the summer, 1942, and ends in April, 1943. Below is a timeline chart for the novel. As you read about an important event, describe it briefly on the "Event" side of the timeline. On the "Reactions" side, explain how the event affects either Phillip or Timothy. The chart has been started for you.

Event August, 1942: Flying boat spots smoke from the cay.	**Event**	**Event**
Reaction The USS *Sedgewick* turns around and rescues Phillip.	**Reaction**	**Reaction**

Event	**Event**	**Event**
Reaction	**Reaction**	**Reaction**

Event	**Event**	**Event**
Reaction	**Reaction**	**Reaction**

Phillip's Story Map

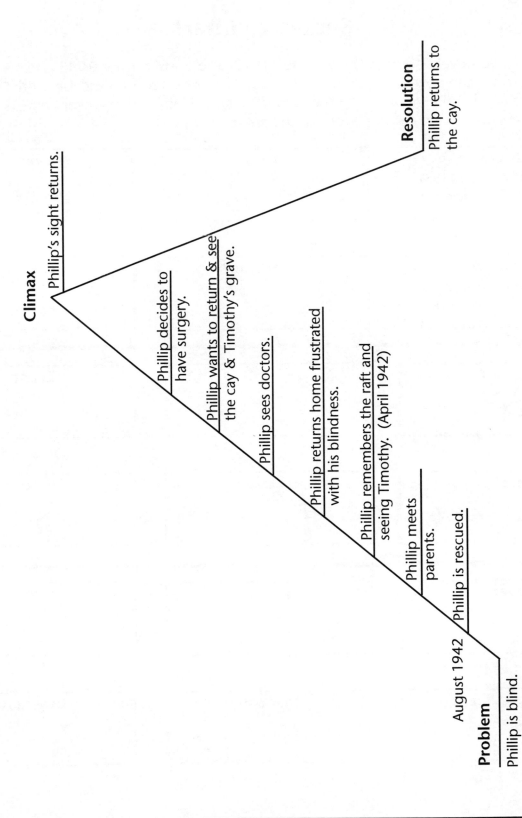

Climax
Phillip's sight returns.

Phillip decides to have surgery.

Phillip wants to return & see the cay & Timothy's grave.

Phillip sees doctors.

Phillip returns home frustrated with his blindness.

Phillip remembers the raft and seeing Timothy. (April 1942)

Phillip meets parents.

Phillip is rescued.

August 1942

Problem
Phillip is blind.

Resolution
Phillip returns to the cay.

Timothy's Story Map

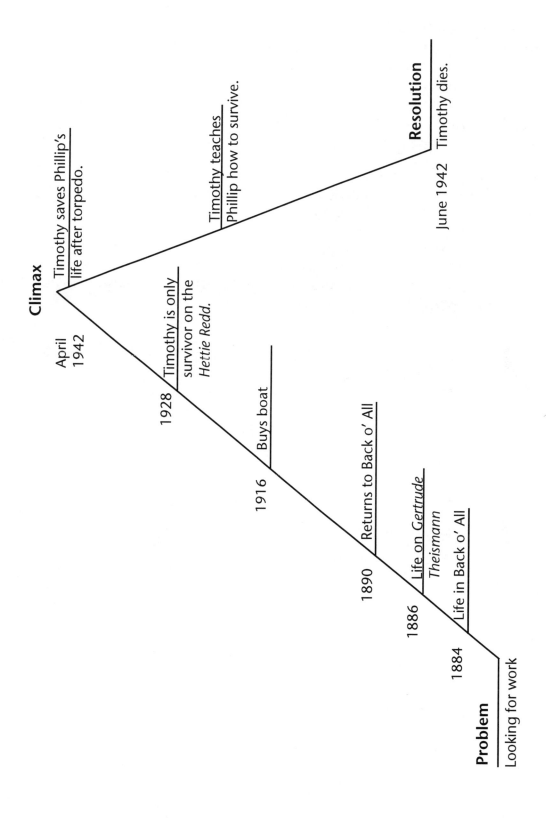

Climax

April 1942 — Timothy saves Phillip's life after torpedo.

1928 — Timothy is only survivor on the *Hettie Redd*.

1916 — Buys boat

1890 — Returns to Back o' All

1886 — Life on *Gertrude Theismann*

1884 — Life in Back o' All

Problem — Looking for work

Timothy teaches Phillip how to survive.

Resolution

June 1942 — Timothy dies.

Recommended Procedure:

This book may be used in several ways: a) read to the entire class; b) read with the class; or c) read in reading groups. It may be read one chapter at a time, using the DRTA, Directed Reading Thinking Activity, Method. This technique involves reading a section, and then predicting what will happen next by making good guesses based on what has already occurred in the story. The predictions are recorded, and verified after the subsequent reading has taken place. (See page 5 of this guide.)

The Discussion Questions and Activities at the end of each chapter, as well as any Postreading Activities and Supplementary Activities, are provided so that you may, using discretion, make selections from them that will be suitable for use by the students in your group.

You may wish to have students show knowledge of words in the vocabulary before reading the chapter by writing simple definitions in their own words. After reading, the students may need to redefine the word by referring to the text and/or dictionary. Additional vocabulary activities are provided.

Using Character Webs—In the Novel Unit Approach

Attribute Webs are simply a visual representation of a character from the novel. They provide a systematic way for the students to organize and recap the information they have about a particular character. Attribute webs may be used after reading the novel to recapitulate information about a particular character or completed gradually as information unfolds, done individually, or finished as a group project.

One type of character attribute web uses these divisions:

● How a character acts and feels. (How does the character feel in this picture? How would you feel if this happened to you? How do you think the character feels?)

● How a character looks. (Close your eyes and picture the character. Describe him to me.)

● Where a character lives. (Where and when does the character live?)

● How others feel about the character. (How does another specific character feel about our character?)

In group discussion about the student attribute webs and specific characters, the teacher can ask for backup proof from the novel. You can also include inferential thinking.

Attribute webs need not be confined to characters. They may also be used to organize information about a concept, object or place.

Attribute Web

The attribute web below is designed to help you gather clues the author provides about what a character is like. Fill in the blanks with words and phrases which tell how the character acts and looks, as well as what the character says and what others say about him or her.

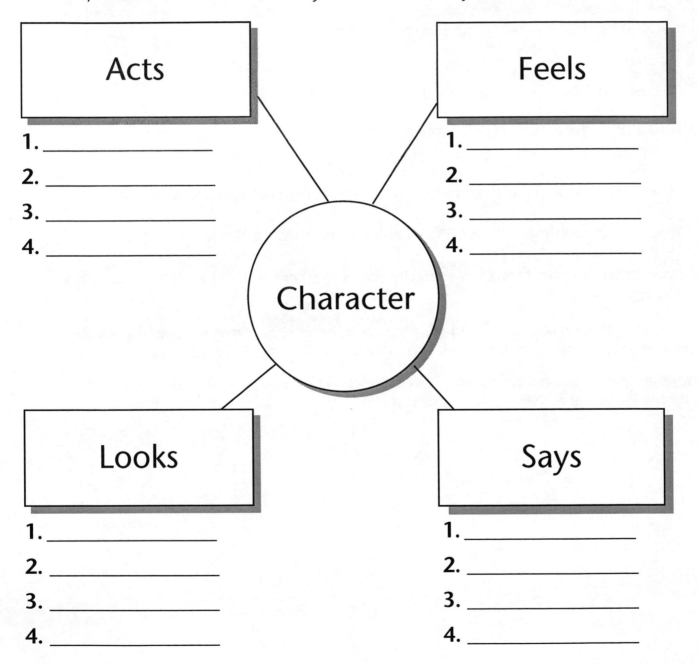

Acts

1. _____
2. _____
3. _____
4. _____

Feels

1. _____
2. _____
3. _____
4. _____

Character

Looks

1. _____
2. _____
3. _____
4. _____

Says

1. _____
2. _____
3. _____
4. _____

Attribute Web

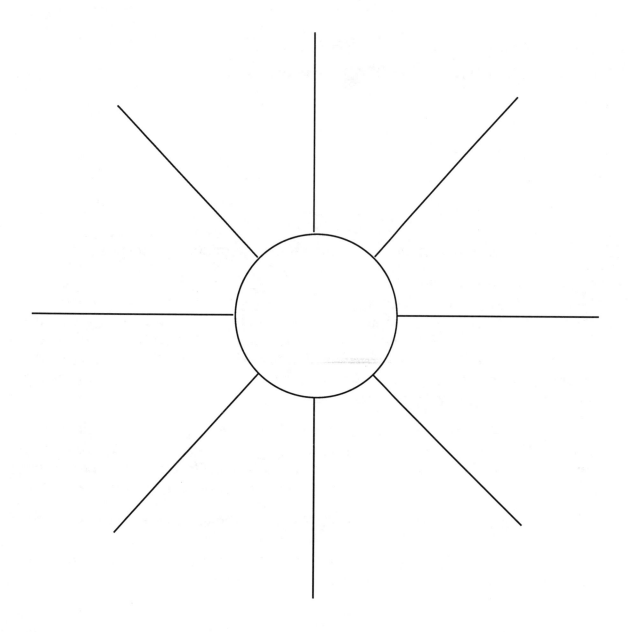

© Novel Units, Inc.

15

Chapter-by-Chapter Vocabulary, Discussion Questions, and Activities

Chapter 1: "USS *Sedgewick*"—Pages 1-7
Chapter 2: "Looking for Work"—Pages 8-14

Vocabulary:

langosta 3	celebrity 6	panicking 7	schooner 8
bark 8	sloop 8	plantain 8	breadfruit 8
mangoes 8	pawpaw 8	sinewy 8	stevedore 9
barrows 9	outrageous 10	bollard 10	mainmast 11
mizzen 11	emancipated 12	surge 12	

Vocabulary Activity:

Sort the vocabulary words into categories: food, seaman terminology, feelings, other.

Discussion Questions and Activities:

1. What is the setting of the opening chapter? *(page 1, sick bay on the hospital of a ship)* What background information does the author supply in the opening paragraph? *(page 1, who the boy was, why he had been lost and his physical condition)* What kind of mood does the author set in only the first page? Does this first page have any effect on you the reader? Is Stew Cat a character in this novel? How important do you think this cat is? Why does the author include him?

2. What was so unusual about Phillip's story? *(Page 2, He survived blind and alone on an island for 47 days.)* How had he managed? *(Page 3, Timothy had prepared him to survive even though he was blind. He had prepared Phillip to get about on the island and to feel comfortable walking around, even though he could not see.)*

3. The Navy found Phillip only by chance. What was the Navy looking for at the time they saw Phillip's fire? *(page 5, a Nazi U-boat)* What do you think would have happened to Phillip if the Navy had not found him? Do you think there was any possibility his vision would have come back on its own?

4. The Navy destroyer was traveling at 25 knots. What did the corpsman mean when he said no torpedo could hit the destroyer? (page 6) Research. (Hint: How fast did torpedoes travel?)

5. Why do you think Phillip wanted to return to the cay? (page 7) Does that make any sense to you?

6. Who was the narrator in Chapter 1? *(Phillip)* In the second chapter the author steps back in time to 1884. Why do you think the author switches the narrator to Timothy and goes back in time? What were the advantages? How does this change in time and narrator help you the reader? Why is this confusing, or is it?

7. What did you learn about Timothy? How old do you think he was in this chapter? How did Timothy as a boy compare to Phillip? How were they alike and different? Use a T-diagram to compare the boys.

Timothy	Phillip
black	white
orphan	two parents
tries to earn money	sheltered only child
healthy	blind

8. What was Timothy's big dream? *(page 10, to own his own schooner or sloop and to be called "Coptin")* How realistic do you think this was? What chance was almost offered to Timothy to become a sailor? *(Pages 10-13, A cabin boy broke his leg and Timothy became his replacement.)*

Prediction:
At the end of Chapter 1, how realistic was Phillip's desire to go back to see the cay after he got his vision back?

At the end of Chapter 2, how realistic was Timothy's hope for his own boat?

Literary Analysis: Dialect—Colloquialism—Point of View—Mood
Dialect is a variety of language that differs from the standard. A dialect is passed down orally and reflects the vocabulary, usage, and pronunciation of a particular region of a country, an ethnic origin, or an occupation. When an author reproduces the sounds, word choices and speech rhythms or characters, he gives an illusion of reality to fictional characters.

Colloquialism is homespun dialect which is passed down orally and reflects the vocabulary, usage, and pronunciation of a particular region. It is used in familiar conversation.

Point of view is the angle from which a narrator tells a story. Who is telling the story? (In some chapters it is Phillip and in others Timothy.) We see and hear only what Phillip or Timothy see and hear.

Mood is the overall emotional atmosphere or feeling of a story, poem or play. An author's choice of setting, language, and writing style help create the mood. The author wants the readers to feel the same way the characters are feeling.

Supplementary Activities:
Geography: Complete the following map activities.

1. Label the following on the map on page 19 of this guide: United States, Panama, Nicaragua, Honduras, St. Thomas, Curacao, and Columbia.

2. Label the following on the map of the world on page 20 of this guide: Africa, United States, South America, England, and France.

3. Mark Timothy's journeys using a colored pencil. Mark the appropriate location of the torpedoing of the *Hato* and the cay. Using a different color pen, mark Phillip's journeys back to Curacao and then to New York. See pages 19 & 20 of this guide.

Chapter 3: "Panama"—Pages 15-20
Chapter 4: "Back o' All"—Pages 21-24
Chapter 5: "The Raft"—Pages 25-26

Vocabulary:

massive 15	subdued 17	taut 17	apprentice 21
galvanized 25	doled 25	hardtack 25	haunches 26

Vocabulary Activity:
Match the vocabulary word with its definition.

Vocabulary Words	Definitions
massive (d)	a. coated
subdued (g)	b. beginner
taut (h)	c. hindquarter
apprentice (b)	d. large
galvanized (a)	e. biscuit
doled (f)	f. handed out
hardtack (e)	g. under control
haunches (c)	h. tense

Discussion Questions and Activities:
1. Phillip's accident had changed his mother. What was she like before the boat was torpedoed? *(pages 17-18, scolding, taut, tense and very frightened of the war and the U-boat attacks)*

2. Phillip called Timothy his guardian angel. What do you think about Phillip talking to Timothy who had died and whom he had buried? Do you think the "sun had fried" Phillip's brain? (page 18)

North and South America

World Map

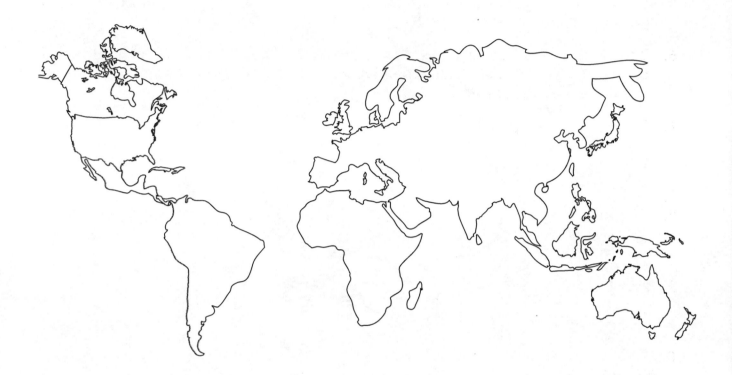

3. What do you think Phillip meant by "pity is often a deadly enemy"? (page 18) Can you give an example of this in your life?

4. Who was Hannah Gumbs? (pages 21-22) Why did she raise Timothy?

5. What do you think the the author meant when he said, "Back o' All smelled of poverty, rain or shine"? (page 21)

6. Why do you think Hannah wanted Timothy to be an apprentice to a wood craftsman? (pages 21-22) Do you think that would have been a safer, better life? Why would a boy rather go to sea as a cabin boy?

7. There are many colloquial expressions in this book. What did Hannah mean when she said, "Don' tie de rope till you cotch de goat"? (page 23) How would you say this? What did she mean by, "Wisdom seldom came out of books"? (page 23) Do you agree or disagree with this?

8. Chapter 5 is a short but very powerful chapter. What does the author tell us about Phillip as a person? *(Page 26, He was a bit prejudiced against black people and he still was little-boy-like. He was not very tough.)*

9. How does the author introduce the problem of the novel? What is the problem? *(Page 26, Phillip had lost his sight and he was alone with a black man and a cat on a raft trying to survive.)*

10. What information about the raft do you think is important? Why would the author include this?

Prediction:
What challenges did Timothy face at the end of Chapter 4? What could happen to him? In contrast, Phillip at the end of Chapter 5 discovered he had lost his sight. What could happen to him?

Literary Analysis: Characterization
Characterization is the way an author informs readers about what characters are like. Direct characterization is when the author describes the character. Indirect characterization is when the reader figures out what the character is like based on what the character thinks, says, or does—and what others say about him.

Which type(s) of characterization does Taylor use to show you what Timothy is like? Phillip? What words and phrases would you use to describe each character? Have students fill in the chart on the next page of this guide.

Characterization

Directions: Characterization is the portrayal of an imaginary person by what he says or does, by what others say about him or how they react to him, and by what the author reveals directly or through a narrator. As you read, look for clues to what a specific character is like. Think about why he/she and others act and speak as they do—and what traits these actions and words reveal. Fill in the chart below to record your ideas.

Character:			
Action/Words	**Reason**	**Trait**	**Narrator's Comments**

Supplementary Activities:
1. Students share their favorite images in this section and examine the various senses to which the imagery appeals.

   Image   **Page**   **Sight**   **Hearing**   **Touch**   **Taste**   **Smell**

2. Writing Idea: Choose a vivid passage from this chapter and write it as a poem. For example, (page 21) "Lye water boiled. Fumes rose from it and lodged in the light, warm rain, clearing nostrils in one whiff. Back o' All smelled of poverty, rain or shine."

Chapter 6: "Shoes"—Pages 27-34
Chapter 7: "Curacao"—Pages 35-43

Vocabulary:

pungent 27	catchment troughs 28	dismay 31	foraged 32
cassava 33	daubed 33	demolished 34	wake 35
acrid 36	convoy 36	ballast 37	

Vocabulary Activity:

List a synonym and an antonym for each word, and then develop word maps for four of the vocabulary words. Compare your word maps with classmates.

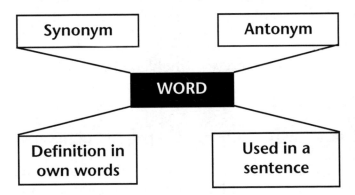

Discussion Questions and Activities:
1. Describe life in Back o' All. What parts of life there would you dislike most? Why did the people in Back o' All think things were not too bad in 1884? (page 28) Have conditions improved for black people on these islands today?

2. What impressed Timothy about the luxury of the ship? *(page 29, the big bed, the bathroom with a sink, toilet and a bathtub)*

3. Why do you think Timothy had never had a pair of shoes before? (page 31) What was good about the shoes? Why did Timothy have problems with them?

4. Why do you think the captain had hired a *bukra* boy and had sailed without telling Timothy? (page 34)

5. In 1942 of Chapter 7, Phillip talked about never having flown before. When did flying for nonmilitary people become ordinary? How many people flew in 1950? In 1960? In 1990?

6. What did Phillip mean by "The darkness held me prisoner"? (page 35) How would you say this? What other things could hold you prisoner?

7. Why did Phillip have mixed feelings about going home? (page 36) What things did he think would be very hard for him to manage? *(page 36, sailing, fishing, going down to the docks by himself)*

8. Why did Phillip become angry and frustrated ? *(Pages 39-40, He became confused in his house and frustrated that his parents didn't just let him make mistakes.)* What did Phillip miss? *(page 41, noises of the wind and the surf, chores and work that made him feel useful, and of course, Timothy)*

Prediction:
At the end of Chapter 6, Timothy watched the ship *Amager* sail off without him. He took off his new shoes and walked home with Hannah. He was disappointed and hurt. What will happen to him?

Phillip in Chapter 7 was home but he too was troubled. He had dreams about Timothy. What could happen to him?

Supplementary Activities:
1. Complete the Critical Thinking Chart. (See page 25 of this guide.)

2. Writing Activity: As Phillip tried to go to sleep, his thoughts went back to life on the cay with Timothy. Describe the friendship between Phillip and Timothy. How did the friendship begin? What did each get from the relationship?

Critical Thinking Chart

Directions: For each character listed in the chart below, indicate how Timothy came into contact with the person, how Timothy felt toward each, and what revelation about life was connected with each character.

Character	Contact	Feelings	Revelation
Hannah Gumbs			
Wobert Avril			
Horace Simpson			
Luther Oisten			
Jennifer Rankin			
Phillip			

Chapter 8: "Being a Slave"—Pages 44-48
Chapter 9: "The Clinic"—Pages 49-51
Chapter 10: "New York City"—Pages 52-56

Vocabulary:

fronds 44   shackled 46   rebellion 46   flared 56

Vocabulary Activity:

Create a picture puzzle for each word. On one side of a card goes a drawing or cutout that represents the word. The player tries to guess the word (printed on the other side). For example, the "shackled" card might show someone in handcuffs. Words from earlier chapters may also be used.

Discussion Questions and Activities:

1. Phillip wanted to know why the *bukras* had left him. How did Hannah answer him? *(pages 44-45)* Why did she tell him about the slave ships?

2. Why did the African chieftains turn over their people to the owners of slave ships? *(Page 45, They traded their people for cheap pots, pans, tools, guns and cheap cloth and jewelry.)* What did the white traders do with the slaves that lived through the terrible trips on the ships? *(Page 46, They sold them to white plantation owners who put the slaves to work in the fields.)*

3. How and when did the slaves get their freedom on Saint Croix? *(Page 47, July 3, 1848. They said they would burn Saint Croix unless they were freed.)* How and when did the slaves in the United States get their freedom? *(1863, Emancipation Proclamation)* What would have happened to the United States slaves if they had rebelled?

4. What was "pidgin Engleesh"? *(page 48)* Is it still used? Where?

5. When is a young person no longer considered a child? Is there a specific age or is it determined by experiences of the person or by society? Do you think Phillip grew up because of his experience on the cay and because of his blindness? How was he like most 12-year-old boys? How did he differ?

6. How have Phillip's father and mother changed since the boat was torpedoed? *(Page 17, His mother was not the tense, taut, scolding woman. Page 51, His father was more forceful since the Hato sinking and he didn't let his wife push him around.)*

7. Why did Phillip want to go up to the top of the Empire State Building? *(Page 54, He wanted to feel the wind.)* How did his mother react? *(Page 54, She didn't think that*

this made sense.) Phillip asked her if she had ever done anything that didn't make sense. Have you ever done something like that? What and under what circumstances? Would you do it again?

8. Phillip talked about some serious issues with his mother. What were the topics and how did this show a certain maturity on Phillip's part? *(pages 55-56, communication with the dead, angels, prejudice, and ideas about integrated neighborhoods)* How did his mother react to Phillip, a grown-up, mature boy? What response from his mother would Phillip have liked? (page 56)

Literary Analysis—Personification:
Personification is a form of figurative language. It occurs when a writer gives human characteristics to an animal or object. Find an example of personification in this section.

Supplementary Activities:
1. Phillip's parents were going through the troubles of his blindness and how that would affect their lives. Write a conversation that they might have had that Phillip would not have been able to overhear.

2. Phillip had some dreams. Some of them were troubling. Describe a dream you have had or one you imagine. It might also be a daydream. Describe what you see, hear, feel, and do in the dream—and how that might help you cope with the problems you are having in real life.

Chapter 11: "Obeah"—Pages 57-63
Chapter 12: "Dr. Pohl"—Pages 64-71
Chapter 13: "The Decision"—Pages 72-73

Vocabulary:
wizened 59	vagrant 59	gullet 63	obeah 63
occipital lobes 65	malformation 65	cauterized 65	vascular 66
hemorrhage 67	acute 67	vegetative 67	residual 69
incapacitated 70			

Vocabulary Activity:
Ask the students to choose the words from this section they think are important to know—and have them tell why.

Discussion Questions and Activities:
1. Timothy did not have a father or grandfather, but what did the old man Wobert teach him? *(Pages 58-60, Answers will vary.)*

2. How was Timothy lucky that he had been born after slavery days? *(Page 60, Life under slavery was hard.)* Was life in Back o' All any better than slavery?

3. What did Wobert mean when he said "black hens lay white eggs" and then "Riddle me dat"? (page 61)

4. What type of person was Mama Geeches? What is an "obeah" woman? *(Page 61, She was paid to chase jumbis and also paid to bring good luck.)* How was she an extortionist? *(Page 62, An extortionist exacts money or something else that is not due, and she tried to get money from Timothy.)* Why did a wise old woman like Tante Hannah believe and fear Mama Geeches? *(Page 63, She used mysterious words, powerful words of magic and everybody feared her and the magic.)*

5. In Chapter 12, Phillip and his parents learned about the possibility of successful surgery. How did Phillip's parents react differently, and why? What did Dr. Pohl mean when he said Phillip was "mentally strong"? (page 68) How do you think you would react in this conversation? Would you want the details of surgery if it were your head and if you were blind? Do you think your parents would let you make such a decision?

6. Phillip recalled Timothy's statements, "No rain, no rainbow," and "Night bring day." (page 72) What do you think Timothy meant? How do you make decisions? Maybe you have never had to make a big decision. How would you do it? Fill out a decision chart for Phillip using a T-diagram.

For Surgery	Against Surgery

7. After Phillip made his decision to have surgery, he said he had to go back to the cay. How were having the surgery and going back to the cay related? Father said Phillip had to have a goal. What do you think he meant? (page 73)

Prediction:
If you were the author of this book, you are at a turning point. What are the possible things that could happen: 1) to Timothy wanting to find a way to sail off? and 2) during Phillip's surgery?

Supplementary Activities:
1. Writing Activity: Describe a time—real or imagined—when you were taken to the hospital. What was your problem? How were you treated? Did you meet other patients?

2. Art: Create a five-frame cartoon strip that shows what happens in one particular episode of the story, such as, when the obeah tries to get Timothy to pay her money. (page 62)

Chapter 14: "Bark *Gertrude Theismann*"—Pages 74-84
Chapter 15: "The Devil's Mouth"—Pages 85-89
Chapter 16: "The Squall"—Pages 90-93

Vocabulary:

laden 74	supple 74	aftermast 75	jibs 75
headsails 75	fo'c'sle 76	bulkhead 76	galley 76
snuff 77	anthracite 77	halyards 77	hawser 78
gypsyheads 78	mizzen crosstrees 78	ratlines 82	shroud 83
holystone 90	royals 91	crojack 91	flying jib 91

Vocabulary Activity:
Create a word wall with a large picture of a ship and the words naming the parts appropriately placed on it.

Discussion Questions and Activities:
1. What is an "idle threat"? (page 75) What are some of the definitions of "idle"? What definition fits with the word "threat"? *(having no power)* Can you think of some "idle threats" you have heard? What kind of power do you think Mama Geeches had over Timothy?

2. Why did Timothy consider life on board the ship "rich-man living"? What was good about boat life? (page 76) What do you consider rich-man living?

3. Why do you think that Captain Roberts didn't tell Timothy the truth about when the boy would return to St. Thomas? Would Timothy have taken the job if he knew the truth? Why or why not?

4. Why did Timothy try to climb the masts before he was ordered? (page 81) How did Timothy make decisions? What went wrong for him? What could have prevented this? *(Page 81, He looked down and froze.)* Have you ever been frightened and froze when you tried climbing?

5. What kind of help did Horace give Timothy? Why do you think he did it? What would have happened if he had not climbed up to Timothy? (page 83) Why did Timothy wonder about the father he had never known?

6. What effect does skipping from Timothy's fear of falling and then his mastery of climbing the masts to Phillip's fear of surgery have on you the reader? How are the two kinds of fear alike and how are they different? What did Phillip and Timothy have in common?

7. When you are nervous about something, how do your parents try to distract you, or what do you think about to become calmer? How did Phillip's parents try to help? *(pages 85-87)* How was their help similar to the help Horace offered Timothy? Why do you think the author created certain types of parallel actions in the two stories of Timothy and Phillip?

8. Do you think it was a good thing that Timothy had his problems climbing on a calm night before he had to climb during the storm? Why or why not? How did Timothy beat Luther Oisten? Why do you think Oisten made him check the ties on the mainroyal when they didn't need it?

Literary Analysis: Conflict
Conflict is a struggle or problem that makes a story interesting. There are several types of conflict: 1) a person against another person, 2) a person against nature or society, and 3) inner conflict, in which a character struggles with his or her own feelings. Ask students to find an example of each type of conflict in *Timothy of the Cay.* (See Supplementary Activity #2 below.)

Prediction:
Timothy was not out of his trouble and neither was Phillip. What could happen to both of them? Do you think the parallel action will continue? In what way?

Supplementary Activities:
1. Make a chart and attribute web of the men on board Timothy's ship.

2. Begin a Nature of Conflict Chart. (See next page of this guide.)

3. Writing: Write the conversation that Timothy might have had with himself about leaving Tante Hannah and going to sea.

4. Drama: Divide the class into groups of two. One will assume the role of Mamma Geeches and the other Timothy. Each person will retell the incident of Mama Geeches' offer to put a spell on the *Amager* and find Timothy a good ship from his point of view. The students will imitate the character with voice and gestures.

The Nature of Conflict

As is true in real life, the characters in novels face many conflicts. When two people or forces struggle over the same thing, conflict occurs. The excitement in novels develops from the use of the three main types of conflict: (1) person against person; (2) person against nature or society; and (3) person against himself or herself.

Below list some of the conflicts from the novel. In the space provided, briefly describe the conflict and indicate which type of conflict is involved, writing "PP" for person vs. person, "PN" for person vs. nature or society, and "PS" for person vs. self. Then choose three of the conflicts and describe how each was resolved.

Conflict	Description	Type

Conflict #1 resolution: _____

Conflict #2 resolution: _____

Conflict #3 resolution: _____

Chapter 17: "My Bald Head"—Pages 94-98
Chapter 18: "Home"—Pages 99-105
Chapter 19: "The Operating Room"—Page 106

Vocabulary:

      malformation 94

Vocabulary Activity:

Using the one vocabulary word, how many words can you make from the letters in three minutes?

Discussion Questions and Activities:

1. Have any of you ever had surgery? Phillip's surgery in 1942 was probably quite different from that same type of surgery today. Hospital procedures are not that different. How did Phillip react to his shaved head? How would you?

2. The author cuts off and switches to the other story of Timothy at an exciting point before Phillip's surgery, leaving the reader up in the air. Why do you think the author does this?

3. What had Timothy learned about his trips around the world? How had he changed? *(page 100)* How do most young men change between 14 and 18 years of age?

4. How did Timothy learn that Hannah had died? What were the colloquial expressions that people used to say that Hannah had died? *(Page 103, "Her lamp done went out." "Her oil gone." Page 104, "Otha side she gone.")*

5. Had Timothy ever considered how much his world in Back o' All could change in four years? How did life in Back o' All look to him? Had he forgotten the smell and the poverty? What beautiful things had he missed? *(pages 100-104)*

6. Do you think dreaming of the cay made it easier for Phillip to face the surgery of boring holes in his head? What do you try to think about when you are troubled? Does it distract or help you? Why?

Prediction:

Timothy was all alone as he faced his future. How will this work out for him?

Phillip, even with all the support of his parents and the hospital people, was alone as he faced his future. What were the possibilities for Phillip? Do you think a 12-year-old really understood all this?

Supplementary Activities:
1. Begin a collage about the images Phillip remembered and what he would like to be able to see again.

2. Respond to the novel by writing a poem. You might choose your favorite passage in the novel and recast it as a poem. You might write a memory poem from Timothy's point of view, a poem that describes the changes in Phillip, an acrostic poem that summarizes the plot or a cinquain about any of the characters. (A cinquain is a poem consisting of five unrhymed lines with respectively two, four, six, eight, and two syllables per line.)

Chapter 20: "The Captain"—Pages 107-112
Chapter 21: "Awakening"—Pages 113-115
Chapter 22: "Jennifer"—Pages 116-124

Vocabulary:

cattacoo 109	careened 110	taffrail 112	wharf 117
ominous 118	helm 119	barometer 120	converged 121
torrential 122			

Vocabulary Activity:
Have the students show knowledge of words before reading the chapter by writing simple definitions in their own words or good guesses of the meanings of the vocabulary words. Ask the students to read for verification or ask students to check their definitions in the dictionary.

Discussion Questions and Activities:
1. What canal had Timothy worked on? *(page 107)* Why was the Panama Canal so important? How much money had Timothy made each year? What were working conditions like? Why do you think Timothy chose to work on the canal rather than on the ships?

2. Why do you think Timothy had many friends who were older men? What was he looking for? *(Opinion–answers may vary. On many occasions, Timothy had looked at older men and wondered what his father was like. He looked to the men as role models or as men who might have been like his father.)*

3. Why do you think Timothy never married? *(Page 108, Timothy believed that men who went to sea didn't make good husbands.)* Why do you think this was so?

4. How did Charlie Bottle help Timothy buy the boat? *(Page 110, Charlie could read and write and was able to talk to the bankers and he could loan him another $200 dollars for the boat.)*

5. At the end of Chapter 20, Timothy was on a high as captain of his own boat. In contrast, how did Phillip feel at the end of Chapter 21?

6. What expression did Mrs. Redd use to say her husband had died? *(Page 116, "De coptin done bus 's rope.)* Why did she ask Timothy for help? Did he have any obligation to help her? *(page 117)*

7. Timothy was superstitious. On what other occasions do you think Timothy was influenced by something other than reason? Why was he hesitant to take his friend's body on the boat? *(page 117)*

8. What were the ominous signs that worried Timothy? *(pages 118-120)* What do you know about hurricanes? Where do they occur? How do ships survive hurricanes?

9. Was there anything that Timothy could have done to prevent the tragedy? *(page 122)* How much responsibility did Timothy have for his passengers' lives?

Prediction:
At the end of Chapter 21, Phillip was very down because he thought the operation had failed. What kind of support did Phillip have? Was there any hope for him?

Literary Analysis: Foreshadowing
Foreshadowing is a hint or suggestion of something that will happen later in a story.

What foreshadowing did the author use in the statement on page 124 about Timothy, "There were dark times ahead, day and night, when he would wish he'd drowned with Jennifer"?

Supplementary Activities:
1. Research the reasons for and the hardships in the construction of the Panama Canal.

2. Research: Where do most hurricanes occur? What is the average and the highest wind speed recorded for hurricanes? What is the difference between a hurricane and and typhoon? What is a tornado? How are these storms alike and how are they different?

Chapter 23: "Trees"—Pages 125-128
Chapter 24: "The *Hato*"—Pages 129-132

Vocabulary:
syndrome 126   hallucinations 126 occipital lobes 127

Vocabulary Activity:
Draw a picture to suggest a vocabulary word. Classmates identify the words. Words from other chapters may be used.

Discussion Questions and Activities:
1. How do you think Phillip felt when he first thought he was seeing trees? What effect did his parents' reactions have on him? *(pages 125-126)* How did the doctor's explanation of Anton's Syndrome help?

2. What part did his hallucination of Timothy play on Phillip? *(page 127)*

3. Why would an old retired sailor like Timothy want to go back to the sea? *(page 131)*

Prediction:
How is the author going to put the two parallel stories of Timothy and Phillip together?

Supplementary Activities:
1. Rewrite Chapter 23 from Phillip's parents' point of view.

2. Select a character or dramatic situation from the novel to paint or draw. Write paragraphs to accompany the drawing which will combine the description of the character and/or the scene.

Chapter 25: "The *Audaz Adventurero*"—Pages 133-135
Chapter 26: "Torpedoed"—Pages 136-140
Chapter 27: "The Cay"—Pages 141-145

Vocabulary:

maneuver 137	fantail 137	menace 137	fore 137
aft 137	indigo 142		

Vocabulary Activity:
Make a poster, banner, or sign to advertise selected vocabulary words.

Discussion Questions and Activities:
1. Phillip's father said a goal would help him go through the surgery and recovery. What if Phillip's sight had not returned? Would he have still wanted to go back to the cay? What did he want to do on the cay?

2. How would you explain or develop what Phillip's father had said about Timothy?

   "Wisdom comes in a lot of varieties." page 134
   "Being intelligent and being wise are two different things." page 135

3. What did we learn about Timothy's shipwreck in the hurricane? *(page 138)* Do you think that it left a lasting impression on him? How was he cleared? Did the favorable inquiry take away his guilt?

4. How did you feel as you read the Germans' version of torpedoing the *Hato*? Since you knew what would happen, did you feel tension?

5. How did seeing the cay help Phillip put his life back together?

Postreading Questions

1. What kind of person would Phillip have become if his boat had not been torpedoed?

2. Setting: What was the advantage of using several settings in this novel?

3. Theme: What was the author's message? Why do you think the author wrote this story? What do you think is the most important thing to remember about this story?

4. Plot: Which parts of this story were most vivid and interesting to you? Choose three events in the story, and write two or three paragraphs about how changing these events would have changed what happened in the story. For example, how might the story have turned out differently if Phillip's operation had not been successful?

5. Character: How did the characters change in this novel? What brought about these changes? Did you find the characters in the book "real"? If so, how did the author bring them to life for you? Select one character in the book who had the qualities of a hero. Make a list of these qualities and tell why he was a hero for you. Does he have qualities you do not admire? How do you justify the hero title when he is not perfect?

6. Do you think the conclusion of the novel is realistic? Could the ending of the novel have been improved? In what way? Write your version of the ending and then share with classmates.

Postreading Activities

Writing

1. Choose another novel about physical disabilities. How are the problems of the central characters alike? How did other people treat the disabled character?

2. Phillip had a dream of returning to the cay. This dream gave him the courage to face the dangerous surgery. Describe a dream or a plan that helped you get through a difficult time. The dream might be one you have really had—or one you imagine. Describe what you see, hear, feel, and do in the dream—and how that helps you cope with the problems you are having in real life.

3. Phillip had to survive on his own. Focus on a time you were pretty much on your own. You solved at least one problem by yourself—because there was no one else to do it. Why were you on your own? What problems arose? What mistakes did you make? Did you learn from them? What did you learn about yourself? Write your story and share with a classmate.

4. "Courage is the thing! All goes if courage goes." Explain whether or not Phillip and/or Timothy's responses support this quote by Sir J.M. Barrie. How did Phillip display courage? Timothy? Both of them were survivors. Was it courage—or something else—that helped them survive?

Writing/ Listening/ Speaking

1. Work with a partner to write an imaginary dialogue between yourself and one of the characters in the novel. The character you choose should act and respond as he or she does in the novel, i.e. Luther Oisten should be cruel, Hannah Gumbs wise and kind, etc. Present the dialogue to your class.

2. Pretend you are a reporter assigned to cover the story of Phillip. Prepare a list of questions you would like to ask. Ask these questions of a group of your classmates. Write the interview for your group.

Language Study

1. Make a list of the 20 vocabulary words you think any reader of this novel should know, and why.

2. Dialect and colloquial expressions play an important part in this novel. Make a list of expressions in dialect/colloquialisms.

Page	Expression	Context Clue	Definition	How you might express idea
23	"Don' tie de rope..."			

Art

1. Illustrate each character in the dress and pose you feel is most characteristic of each.

2. Create a mobile based on the important objects or ideas in the novel.

3. Create a poster to advertise a movie version of the story.

Bibliography

Books on Ships and Sailing:

Blackburn, Graham. *The Illustrated Encyclopedia of Ships, Boats, Vessels, and Other Waterborn Craft.* Overlook, 1978.

Chant, Christopher. *Sailing Ships.* Marshall Cavendish, 1989. Clear, detailed pictures are the highlight of this history of sailing ships.

Rutland, Jonathan P. *Ships.* Rev. ed. Watts, 1981.

Whipple, Addison B. C. *The Challenge: A History of Clipper Ships.* Morrow, 1987.

Assessment for *Timothy of the Cay*

Assessment is an on-going process, more than a quiz at the end of the book. Points may be added to show the level of achievement. When an item is completed, the teacher and the student check it.

Name _____ Date _____

Student	Teacher		
_____	_____	1.	Keep a reaction journal for each chapter of the novel.
_____	_____	2.	Complete the map activities marking the United States, Panama, Nicaragua, Honduras, St. Thomas, Curacao, and Colombia.
_____	_____	3.	Complete the Characterization Chart on page 22 of this guide.
_____	_____	4.	Writing Activity: Phillip had some dreams. Some of them were troubling. Describe a dream you have had or one you imagine. It might also be a daydream. Describe what you see, hear, feel, and do in the dream—and how that helps you cope with the problems you are having in real life.
_____	_____	5.	Art: Create a five-frame cartoon strip that shows what happens in one particular episode of the story, such as when the obeah tries to get Timothy to pay her money.
_____	_____	6.	Make a chart and attribute web for the men on board Timothy's ship.
_____	_____	7.	With a partner, assume the role of Mama Geeches or Timothy. Each person will retell the incident of Mama Geeches' offer to put a spell on the *Amager* from his/her point of view. Imitate the character with voice and gestures.
_____	_____	8.	Make a collage about the images Phillip remembers and what he would like to be able to see again.

_____   _____   9. Choose your favorite passage in the novel and recast it as a poem. You might write a memory poem from Timothy's point of view, a poem that describes the changes in Phillip, an acrostic poem that summarizes the plot, or a cinquain about any of the characters.

_____   _____   10. Make a list of the 20 vocabulary words you think any reader of this novel should know—and why.

Comments: